D1103471

WORLD WAR II
IN PHOTOGRAPHS

WORLD WAR II
IN PHOTOGRAPHS

SERIES EDITOR PAUL WHITTLE

EAGLE EDITIONS

Acknowledgements

Thanks are due to the following people for making this book possible: Thomas Mitchell for picture research; Andrew Webb at the Robert Hunt Library for his indefatigable search for the right pictures; Hulton Getty Images Ltd; Matthew Smith and all at Arcuturus, rising star in the publishing firmament; Jonathan Watts, inspirational historian; Heike Becker for being there; Annette Krzyworaczka, for being the best.

Published by Eagle Editions Limited
11 Heathfield, Royston, Hertfordshire SG8 5BW

All rights reserved. No part of this publication may be reproduced, stored in a retrieval system, or transmitted, in any form or by any means, electronic, mechanical, photocopying, recording or otherwise, without written permission in accordance with the provisions of the Copyright Act 1956 (as amended). Any person or persons who do any unauthorized act in relation to this publication may be liable to criminal prosecution and civil claims for damages.

Published 2003

© Arcturus Publishing Limited
26/27 Bickels Yard
151–153 Bermondsey Street
London SE1 3HA

Series jacket design by Alex Ingr
Designed and Typeset by Mike Harrington,
MATS Typesetting

ISBN 1-84193-193-4

Printed and bound in China

Contents

INTRODUCTION: BETWEEN THE WARS 1919–1936

THE FIRST AND SECOND WORLD WARS have been described as a single war with a long pause for breath in the middle. While this is perhaps something of an exaggeration, it is undeniably true that the seeds of what would become the Second World War were sown in the aftermath of the First.

When the armistice of November 1918 was signed, Germany possessed over 200 divisions on the front line in the West, with a further 70 occupying the territory gained from Russia in the East. The legend soon grew that Germany had not been defeated in the field, but had in fact been 'stabbed in the back' by communists and traitors back at home: the so-called '*Dolchstoss*' legend. The embittered front-line troops returning home found a battered and dispirited nation, with many cities in the hands of 'Workers' Councils', set up on the Soviet model. Many servicemen banded together into what became known as the '*Freikorps*', an unofficial rightist militia, and took it upon themselves to restore order to the nation. The fledgling socialist government, lacking troops of its own, was forced to use these groups to combat communist occupation of cities, earning itself little respect from either Left or Right.

At this point, a newly-demobbed Corporal Adolf Hitler was working for army intelligence assessing 'radical elements', one of which was the *Deutsche Arbeiter Partei* (DAP), the German Workers' Party. Attracted by their anti-Semitic, anti-capitalist stance, and also their lack of an established leader, Hitler became Party Member 555 (not number 7, as he would later claim), and quickly took over the party, renaming it the *National Sozialist Deutsche Arbeiter Partei*, (NSDAP), abbreviated to Nazi Party.

◆ The signing of the Armistice, November 1918. The German surrender of 1918 was widely regarded as a national humiliation by a people that believed itself undefeated in the field, a belief encouraged by the self-serving memoirs published by senior generals such as Erich Ludendorff. In fact, Germany was militarily and economically exhausted, and if it had not negotiated a peace in 1918, would have been utterly crushed in 1919.

◆ *Freikorps* unit on the streets in Germany, c. 1920. The post-war years were lawless ones in Germany, with both extreme Left and Right battling for control of the local city and state governments. The *Freikorps* units were mostly made up of disenchanted ex-soldiers, of a decidedly right-wing bent.

➡ Hitler speaks at the first gathering of flag and standard bearers of the Nazi Party on the Marsfeld in Munich, 28 February 1923.

◗ Nazi gathering in Munich, May Day, 1923. The expected battle with Communists failed to materialise when police, forewarned of the Nazis' intentions, herded them on to the Theresienwiese, open land near the city, and held them there for the rest of the day.

◗ The 'Beer Hall Putsch', 9 November 1923. The attempt to take over the Bavarian government came to nothing when police opened fire on the putschists, which included Hitler and the First World War hero General Ludendorff. Fourteen of the 'putschists' were killed, including Hitler's bodyguard Ulrich Graf, and another close confidant of Hitler Erwin Sheubner-Richter.

➧ Ludendorff and Hitler (front, second and third from right) at the trial subsequent to the failed November Putsch. Röhm of the SA is on the extreme right.

◀ Captain Ernst Röhm, leader of the SA. An original Nazi believer, this tough little ex-captain had emigrated to South America after the failure of the November Putsch in Munich, where he joined the Bolivian Army. In 1930 after a personal appeal from Hitler he returned to become head of the SA and of the SS. It was Röhm's espousal of the continuation of the Nazi 'revolution from below', coupled with his insistence that the SA should be built up as a rival power base to the army that led to his downfall in the Night of the Long Knives, in June 1934.

➡ Stormtroopers parade through the streets of Germany, circa 1932. By this time, the Nazis had a considerable following, and Hitler was just months away from the Chancellorship of Germany.

⬥ Day of Potsdam, 21 March 1933. The newly-appointed Chancellor Hitler greets President Paul von Hindenburg at the opening of the new German parliament at Potsdam, the old capital of Prussia.

◆ (Left to right) Otto von Meissner, chief of the Presidential Chancellery, Vice Chancellor Franz von Papen, Minister of Defence General von Blomberg, Chancellor Hitler and Goebbels in a photograph taken on May Day 1933, months after Hitler's elevation to the chancellorship.

◆ Stormtroopers lead the Nazi boycott of Jewish business in Berlin, 1 April 1933.

The November Putsch and beyond

In 1923, inspired in part by the Italian Fascist 'March on Rome', Hitler made an attempt to take over the Bavarian government as a prelude to a 'March on Berlin', in which the war hero Ludendorff also took part. This sad little affair came to nothing, but during the subsequent trial, Hitler was given a platform in court from which to speak, where he stressed his patriotism, his belief in the 'German Revolution', and his conviction that the army should be rebuilt in opposition to the terms of the Versailles Treaty, a conviction noted by many army officers. Improvements in economic conditions meant interest in radical parties waned, but the Crash of 1929 plunged the nation into economic chaos, and left millions unemployed: fertile ground for Hitler's own particular brand of racist-nationalist, anti-democratic rhetoric. Always the most credible far-Right party (most of the others being more interested in internal power struggles than in actually launching a serious bid for political power), the Nazis and in particular the brown-shirted stormtroopers, the *Sturmabteilungen* (SA), led by ex-Reichswehr captain Ernst Röhm, exerted a powerful attraction on ex-soldiers. This appeal would spread to the middle classes, who felt themselves marginalised by the conservative establishment and the proletarian workers' parties. By 1933, the Nazis were a large and powerful political force in the Reichstag, backed by the three-million-strong SA, who could deliver physical control of the streets. The conservative Right, believing that Hitler could be used and then ignored, installed him as Chancellor, although he had no majority in the 1933 elections: he was never, as is often claimed, democratically elected. Within the space of a few months, Hitler had outmanoeuvred his opponents and had sole control of the German state. The army's cooperation with the SS (the black-shirted *Schutzstaffeln*, originally formed as bodyguards to the Nazi leadership) during the 'Blood Purges' of the Night of the Long Knives, brought it ever closer to Hitler, if to an extent unwillingly. After Hindenburg's death, the loyalty oath sworn by the army to the President as commander-in-chief and head of state became an oath to Hitler personally. Although many sections of the army disapproved of Hitler, they were in whole-hearted agreement with his rearmament of Germany, his expansion of the military, and the reintroduction of compulsory military service. By 1936, Hitler was ready to flex his new military muscle.

🔺 Ernst Röhm in conversation with Kurt Daluege at an SS gathering in Berlin, August 1933.
Daluege was Reinhard Heydrich's second in command at the Nazi Security Service, the SD. As 'Protector' of
Bohemia on Heydrich's assassination in May 1942, Daluege was responsible for the massacre of the Czech village
of Lidice in reprisal. Convicted of war crimes by a Czech court, Daluege was hanged in Prague in 1946.
Looking on from behind is *SS-Reichsführer* Heinrich Himmler, possibly already contemplating Röhm's removal
in the Night of the Long Knives, 30 June 1934.

SECTION II: THE ROAD TO WAR 1936–1939

IN 1936, A FEW MONTHS after the coal-producing region of the Saarland in southern Germany had voted overwhelmingly in a plebiscite to return to Germany, Hitler turned his attention to the demilitarised zone of the Rhineland, and on 7 March 1936, German troops were ordered to occupy the area. Hitler's generals, including Blomberg and Jodl, were nervous of the French reaction, and had given the troops explicit orders to retreat back across the Rhine at the first sign of French opposition. The opposition never came, and Hitler, who had refused the generals permission to withdraw, found his hand enormously strengthened in the struggle for effective control of the armed forces.

In 1936, Italy invaded Abyssinia (modern-day Ethiopia). The League of Nations, the forerunner to the United Nations, condemned the invasion, prompting the Italians to withdraw from the League. Hitler himself had withdrawn from the League on his accession to power in 1933, and was only too eager to welcome Italy into the Anti-Comintern Pact in September 1937, a move which brought the two dictators ever closer.

In 1937 Defence Minister General von Blomberg married his secretary, Eva Gruhn, a woman who, it turned out, had a past as a prostitute and pornographic model (a fact that may have been known to Göring, but one which he did not reveal to Blomberg until after the wedding). On

Blomberg's resignation in early 1938, his obvious successor was the Commander-in-Chief of the Army General von Fritsch. However, Fritsch had made little secret of his contempt for the Nazi Party, and the SS in particular. Days later, he too was got out of the way, the victim of a convoluted homosexual scandal cooked up by Himmler and his sidekick Heydrich. It was time for another radical shake-up of the German officer class, Hitler decided. The Ministry of Defence was abolished, replaced with the High Command of the Armed Forces, the *Oberkommando der Wehrmacht (OKW)*. Hitler appointed himself Commander-in-Chief of the Armed Forces in Blomberg's stead, and appointed General von Brauchitsch, a weak, vacillating character, to Commander-in-Chief of the Army. He also took the opportunity to relieve sixteen other high-ranking generals, including Rundstedt, Leeb, Witzleben, Kluge and Kleist, of their commands, albeit temporarily. The German officer corps stood by and watched as it became totally subordinate to the person of the Führer. The Nazi revolution was complete. Attention could now be turned to the quest for *Lebensraum* (living space) for the Greater German Reich.

◆ Hitler and Mussolini, Munich, September 1937. Italy has just joined Germany and Japan in the Anti-Comintern Pact, agreeing not to support the Soviet Union in any attack on each other's countries.

The first move towards creating this Reich would be the annexation of Austria, the largest German-speaking territory outside of Germany itself, and Hitler's homeland. This *Anschluss* took place in March 1938, to the general enthusiasm of the Austrian public.

With the creation of the *Waffen-SS* (Armed SS) in August 1938, Hitler's assurances to the army that they would remain the sole armed force in Germany, assurances that had ensured the complicity of the army in the reduction of the SA, were shown to be hollow.

The Nazis now turned their attention was Czechoslovakia. An area of western Czechoslovakia, known as the Sudetenland, contained large numbers of ethnic Germans, parcelled into Czechoslovakia together with remnants of the Austro-Hungarian Empire at the end of the First World War. At the instigation of the Germans, Nazi sympathisers in the Sudetenland began political agitation, claiming discrimination by the Czech state. Hitler was again able to portray this as an international crisis, and threaten military intervention to ensure that no 'German blood would be spilled'.

◀ German troops cross into the Rhineland 7 March 1936. After the First World War, this area of Germany was demilitarised and set up as a 'buffer zone' between France and Germany. Its reoccupation by a token German force was a key moment in the power struggle between Hitler and his generals on the one hand, and Hitler and the governments of France and Britain on the other.

At the Munich conference on 29 September, the 'Four Powers' of Germany, Italy, France and Great Britain agreed to the German occupation of all areas with a higher than fifty per cent concentration of ethnic Germans, effectively dismembering the fledgling Czech state. Hitler had once again achieved his stated aim without recourse to war, convincing the German people that he had no intention of going to war. In March 1939, however, the German army occupied the last Czech provinces of Bohemia and Moravia, turning them into a 'Protectorate', later to fall under the command of Himmler's sidekick Reinhard Heydrich. In the same month, the area of Memel was also annexed from Lithuania. Although these actions were in flagrant breach of the Munich Agreement, they took place against a deafening diplomatic silence from both France and Great Britain. However, when Hitler turned his attention to the city of Danzig, and the 'Polish Corridor', it finally became clear that appeasement was no longer a viable policy. Hitler had by now become openly contemptuous of France and Great Britain, and on 27 April he repudiated the Anglo-German Naval Agreement, which had kept the German Navy at an agreed proportion of the Royal Navy for the previous four years. The heavy cruiser *Admiral Hipper* was commissioned the following day; within a few months, German submarines and warships began to sail from port to take up their battle stations in the North Atlantic and the Baltic.

On 23 August the Non-Aggression Pact between the USSR and Germany was signed in Moscow by Ribbentrop and Molotov, in which each nation agreed not to attack the other, and recognised the other's sphere of influence in the Baltic. Secret protocols agreed on the partitioning of Poland upon a German invasion. In this way, Hitler hoped to localise the Polish invasion, which had been planned for months.

On the eve of the invasion of Poland, Hitler hesitated, in part due to the urgings of practically all his highest generals. What was the British reaction likely to be? This was in the light of the treaty signed in March, which guaranteed that Britain, together with France, would give the Polish government 'all support in their power' in the event of any attack on Poland. On 1 September 1939, however, the invasion of Poland went ahead as planned. After British and French acquiescence in the military occupations of the Rhineland, Austria, the Sudetenland, Bohemia and Moravia, and Memel, Hitler was convinced that they would back down once more over the question of Poland. He was wrong.

▶ The High Command of the Wehrmacht. Fritsch (centre) and von Blomberg (right), seen here with Field Marshal von Rundstedt. With the engineered dismissal of these two officers, unopposed by the officer corps, Hitler tightened his control of the army.

◀ Field Marshal Wilhelm Keitel, chief of Hitler's High Command (*Oberkommando der Wehrmacht*). Nicknamed *Lakeitel* – toady – by his contemporaries for his fawning behaviour towards Hitler, Keitel would end his military career on the gallows at Nuremberg.

➤ Vienna, Austria, 22 February 1938. Nazi students from the University of Vienna demonstrate in favour of political union with Germany. The demonstration was quickly broken up by police, but the point had been made.

Reading the results of the Austrian plebiscite are (left to right) Propaganda Minister Josef Goebbels, Hitler and Deputy Führer Rudolf Hess. The Austrian people have voted to endorse Anschluss by an overwhelming majority of around 99.7%. Whether the vote can be said to have been held under free and fair conditions is another matter.

Salzburg, Austria, 13 March 1938. The entry of German troops into Austria during the Anschluss is greeted jubilantly by the city's inhabitants.

◀ Copies of *Der Sturmer*, a virulently anti-Semitic magazine published by Julius Streicher on sale in a German street, c. 1937. The headline reads 'Murderers from the beginning'. Note also the swastika bedecked tram in the background.

➤ Heinrich Himmler

In August 1938, the *Waffen-SS*, the 'Armed SS' was set up by Hitler and Himmler (seen above, at a speech made in the town of Dachau). It was in effect the Nazi private army, answerable only to the Führer. Its main aim was to function as a rival to the *Wehrmacht*, and to provide protection for the Nazis in the unlikely event of an army coup.

➤ Party rally in Berlin, 9 September 1938.

◆ Neville Chamberlain heads home from the Munich Peace Conference, September 29, 1938, accompanied by an SS guard of honour, and Hitler's Ambassador to Great Britain, Baron von Ribbentrop. A vain, arrogant and above all stupid man, Ribbentrop was a disaster as British ambassador, greeting King George V with a '*Heil Hitler*' at a reception. Ribbentrop's personal enemy, Herman Göring, was highly critical of his appointment to the post. Hitler defended Ribbentrop's appointment, saying that Ribbentrop knew 'Lord So and So and Minister So and So'. Göring replied, 'Yes, but the difficulty is that they know Ribbentrop'.

◆ (Left to right)Neville Chamberlain, French Premier Edouard Daladier, Hitler, Mussolini, and Italian Foreign Minister Count Ciano at the signing of the Munich Agreement, 29 September 1938. Under the terms of the agreement, Germany is to mount a 'token' occupation of the Czech Sudetenland, to be followed by a plebiscite. Representatives of the Czech government were not invited to the conference.

🔺 Staged propaganda photograph, showing the entry of German troops into the Sudetenland, October 1938.

🔻 *Reichskristallnacht* (Night of Broken Glass), 9. 11. 1938. Jewish businesses across the length and breadth of Germany were vandalised, as were synagogues and Jewish homes, to the evident approval of at least some of the German public.

Crossing the Charles Bridge, Prague, 15 March 1939. The German occupation of the rump of the Czech state convinces most observers that there is no limit to Hitler's territorial ambitions. His seizure of Memel in Lithuania later that same month would confirm this.

Destroyed synagogue in the Baltic city of Danzig. Separated from the greater part of Germany after the First World War, the inhabitants of Danzig had never really accepted the city's status, and were among the most enthusiastic supporters of Nazism.

German officers share a joke with a disarmed Czech guard at Prague Castle. The expressions of jollity seem somewhat forced, however.

SECTION III: THE AXIS ASCENDANT
SEPTEMBER 1939–JUNE 1942

1. Opening Moves

CASE WHITE: THE GERMAN INVASION OF POLAND

On 1 September 1939, in response to a staged Polish attack on a German radio station faked by Heydrich of the *SD* (*Sicherheitsdienst*, the Nazi security service), a force of 1.5 million German troops, divided into Army Group North under General Fedor von Bock, and Army Group South under General Gerd von Rundstedt rolled across the 1,250-mile Polish border. The invading force was made up of some 62 German divisions, including six Panzer and ten motorised divisions, supported by over 1,200 aircraft concentrating on ground support for the troops rather than on bombing cities. It was this all-arms approach that made the Werhmacht the modern fighting force that it was. Although the

⬆ German field gun moves up an avenue of trees during the Polish campaign, September 1939.

Poles had nearly as many infantry troops as the Germans, they were vastly outnumbered in terms of tanks, artillery and aircraft, and were tactically inferior to the German invaders. The British deadline for a German withdrawal ran out at 9.00 a.m. on 3 September, and at 11.00 a sombre Chamberlain announced to the British nation that they were now at war with Germany for the second time in three decades. The French declaration of war followed at 5.00 p.m. the same day. Neither country was in the least prepared for war, however, and as a consequence were utterly unable to commit any troops to the defence of Poland, or to attack Germany itself across the Rhine. The outnumbered Poles fought gallantly, but by 27 September Warsaw had surrendered. The Soviets had also committed two fronts (army groups) to attacking Poland from the east, and by October Poland had been split between the two attackers, and had effectively ceased to exist. The Polish government, however, had escaped to Romania, and thence to London, where they would continue the fight from exile. Around 100,000 troops also escaped, including airmen who would join their exiled

◆ Polish officers surrender outside Lemberg.

government in Britain and play a vital role in the Battle of Britain during spring 1940. Bravely though the Polish army had fought, it was simply outclassed by the modernised German army, particularly the Panzer divisions developed by General 'Fast Heinz' Guderian. The Wehrmacht would outclass more European armies before it was finished. The tactical doctrines advocated by the German generals such as Erich von Manstein and Heinz Guderian had resulted in the development of separate Panzer divisions, comprising tanks, artillery, anti-tank weaponry and motorised tank support infantry, and heavily supported from the air by ground-attack aircraft such as the Junkers 87, the Stuka. These divisions would punch through enemy lines and encircle the enemy troops in what were known as *Kesseln*, (cauldrons), where they would be attacked from all sides and quickly destroyed. The speed at which the armoured divisions operated led the British to coin the phrase *Blitzkrieg*, lightning war. Although the concept would not be fully developed until Operation *Barbarossa*, the invasion of Russia in June 1941, it would prove effective against France and the British Expeditionary Force in June 1940.

♦ Polish prisoners with their German captors.

◆ Hitler pays a visit to the besieging troops around Warsaw, September 1939.

◆ The German entry into Warsaw is watched by Hitler and his generals.

◗ The Wehrmacht enters Warsaw via one of the city's bridges, 28 September 1939. The Polish campaign had lasted just four weeks, although it had cost the Germans around 50,000 casualties, including 15,000 dead.

◆ Street in Warsaw, October 1939, showing the devastation left in the wake of the German invasion. Scenes like this would become common around the world for the next six years.

◆ Russian troops occupy eastern Poland, in accordance with secret protocols contained within the Nazi-Soviet Pact of 1939.

RUSSO-FINNISH WINTER WAR NOVEMBER 1939–MARCH 1940

The Red Army, unlike the Wehrmacht, had not modernised especially well, particularly in the area of tactics, and this became apparent in November 1939. Flushed with success in Poland, Stalin decided that the time was right for a little empire-building of his own. In November 1939 the Soviet Union attacked its neighbour to the west, Finland. The Finns exploited the tactical ineptness of the Soviets to score some spectacular victories, particularly at Suomussalmi, but they could not follow them up, and the Red Army was able to regroup. By March 1940 the so-called Winter War was over, leaving the Russians with substantial territorial gains, and the Finns looking for an alliance with Nazi Germany.

⬆ Finnish ski troops use reindeer to haul their supplies and equipment during the Winter War against the Soviet Union.

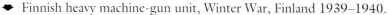

⬅ Finnish heavy machine-gun unit, Winter War, Finland 1939–1940.

The Phoney War September 1939–April 1940

After the fall of Poland came a period of relative quiet. The French reinforced the Maginot Line, their huge defensive wall along their border with Germany. The British Expeditionary Force, initially consisting of four divisions, eventually to increase to nine, arrived in France in October. This period of inactivity was dubbed 'sitzkrieg', or the Phoney War by the British press, and the strange atmosphere of being at war without actually being involved in fighting is well captured in Evelyn Waugh's novel *Put Out More Flags*. On 9 April, however, Hitler made his next move: the invasion of Denmark and Norway. Denmark surrendered on the same day, but the Norwegian will to resist was stiffer, enabling them to hold out, with assistance from Britain and France until June. By this time, however, the German assault on the Netherlands and France had begun, and Allied attention was quickly drawn to this new theatre of conflict. Narvik in northern Norway was the last town to fall, holding out until 9 June, when it was abandoned after being deliberately destroyed.

▶ German airlanding troops on the march to occupy military installations, at Aalborg in northern Denmark 9 April 1940.

➥ The Wehrmacht occupies Kastrup Aerodrome, in Copenhagen, Denmark.

◗ German warship in Oslo harbour, April 1940.

◗ Troops disembark at Oslo as the Germans occupy southern Norway. The north would hold out for several more weeks before finally capitulating.

2. War in the West, May–June 1940

By the time Narvik fell, the Netherlands and Belgium had surrendered, the British Expeditionary Force had come perilously close to being captured en masse at Dunkirk before its spectactular evacuation, and the Wehrmacht stood before the gates of Paris.

The Allies had expected the Germans to repeat the Schlieffen Plan of the First World War and attack through Belgium and northern France. Consequently, this was where most of their troop strength was to be based, on the assumption that the Maginot Line would be strong enough to hold the German advance, and that the heavily-wooded country of the Ardennes was impassable. The Ardennes, however, turned out to be very much passable, and on 10 May 1940 this was exactly where the main German assault came. Spearheaded by the elite *Panzergruppen* of General Guderian, von Rundstedt's Army Group A had broken through in the Ardennes, pushed across France, and reached the Channel port of Calais by 22 May, less than two weeks after the initial attack. Five days later advanced Panzer units reached the British perimeter around Dunkirk, where they were given the order to halt, an order that came directly from Hitler. There has been much debate amongst historians, not to mention the generals involved,

☛ German infantry cross French barbed wire, May 1940.

as to why this order was given. Explanations have ranged from Hitler's belief that the British would negotiate a peace if treated magnanimously, to disputing that the order to halt actually came from Hitler, to a belief that the British would join the Nazi war against Bolshevism. One recent theory, which may be the most accurate, is that on Hitler's maps the country around Dunkirk was marked as being flooded at this time of year, and Hitler's own remembrances of the mud of Flanders persuaded him not to risk the precious Panzers. Whatever the reason, the evacuation of the troops from Dunkirk in the famous 'army of little ships' was regarded back in

Britain as little short of miraculous, and the 'Dunkirk spirit' would pass into legend. Meanwhile, the Germans took Paris on 14 June, after heavy fighting, and by 25 June the German front was just north of the line Bordeaux–Limoges–Grenoble. The French government had little choice but to seek terms of surrender, and the agreement was signed in the same railway carriage at Compiegne where the 1918 Armistice had been signed. What the armies of the Kaiser had failed to take in four years, Hitler now occupied after just six weeks. With one enemy in the west out of the way, he now turned his attention to the other.

◀ German armoured spearheads advance towards the Channel ports, May 1940.

◆ Motorised infantry move up in support of a Panzer division. Mobility was to prove the key to German military success.

◆ Motorcyclists of a motorised division take a break.

◆ General 'Fast Heinz'
Guderian, the soldier who more
than any other developed tank
tactics and the concept of fast-
moving armoured units supported
by motorised infantry and ground-
attack aircraft: *Blitzkrieg*.

◗ German soldiers watch
as Rotterdam burns in
the background.

◀ The French city of
Rouen burns during the
German invasion.

German machine gun post, France 1940.

☛ German Panzer II makes its way down the Champs-Elysee, Paris 14 June 1940. Although this type of tank was inferior to the French and British models in use at the time, the German use of the tanks, including a radio in each one and a two-man turret, obviating the need for the commander to load and fire the gun, was superior.

◀ Watched by a lone French policeman, German troops parade underneath Napoleon's Arc de Triomphe: this was not the sort of triumph Napoleon had in mind when he ordered the Arc to be built.

🔺 The British Expeditionary Force queues up at Dunkirk to be evacuated by the 'little ships': any remotely seaworthy craft was sailed across the Channel by civilians to pick up the country's soldiers.

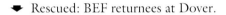

🔻 Rescued: BEF returnees at Dover.

🔻 British troops on the pier at Dunkirk.

3. Britain Stands Alone

OPERATION *SEALION*

With the defeat of France and the humbling of the British Expeditionary Force, Hitler thought that Britain would soon come to the negotiating table. He had never intended a war with Britain, realising that a British defeat would mean the breakup of the British Empire, which he did not regard as being in Germany's best interest. He found, however, that he had misjudged the British reaction to German military success, which was not compliance but defiance. He therefore ordered his generals to start putting into action the plan for the invasion of Britain, codenamed Operation *Sealion*, the name reflecting its maritime nature. However, there was soon disagreement between the army and the navy, with the army demanding the broadest possible front of attack, stretching from Lyme Bay to Ramsgate, a distance of over two hundred miles. This, the navy believed, in the teeth of attacks by the RAF and the Royal Navy, would be suicide. Their proposed solution, however, a front between Folkestone and Eastbourne (a distance of around fifty miles) was angrily rejected by the Army Chief of Staff, General Franz Halder, with the terse comment that he might as well put his men through a sausage machine.

➤ Rehearsing Operation *Sealion*, the Nazi plan for the invasion of Britain. A German half-track is prepared to be driven ashore.

THE BATTLE OF BRITAIN JULY–OCTOBER 1940

At the outset of the German attempt to destroy the aerial superiority of the RAF, the Luftwaffe possessed 2,800 aircraft, fighters and bombers, against the 700 fighters of the RAF. Concentrating on attacking British ports and shipping did little damage to the British war effort, and so the Germans switched to attacking airfields, radar stations and central command installations. This was infinitely more successful, and by early September British aircraft losses were running almost equal to those of the Luftwaffe, and more crucially, the RAF was running low on pilots. At this point, the outlook was bleak; however, another change in emphasis, this time to the terror bombing of British cities in retaliation for an RAF strike on Berlin, gave Fighter Command time to regroup. By October, the Battle of Britain was over. The 'Few' had prevailed.

▲ German half-track is driven ashore from a landing craft during the planning of Operation *Sealion*. Watching are Wehrmacht soldiers, and two sailors of the Kriegsmarine filming the whole spectacle. The operation was called off after the Luftwaffe failed to destroy the Royal Air Force in the Battle of Britain.

Reichsmarschall Hermann Göring, Head of the Luftwaffe. The last leader of the famous First World War *Jagdstaffel Richthofen*, the squadron of the 'Red Baron' Manfred von Richthofen, Göring proved less competent at a higher level of command.

German Heinkel III bombers approach the English coast.

◆ Supermarine Spitfires of 19 Squadron at Duxford Aerodrome, shown here before the outbreak of the war. The Spitfire, with its cruising speed of over 350mph, and high manoeuvrability, was to play a crucial role in the success of the Battle of Britain.

◆ Dornier D17s on their way to attack England, August 1940.

Dogfight over the Kent coast. The vapour trails show the flight paths of the aircraft and also graphically demonstrate the need for manoeuvrability in fighter aircraft.

RAF pilot on night duty at an Eastern Counties aerodrome. Dressed in full flying gear, and with flight bag to hand, he is ready to scramble instantly.

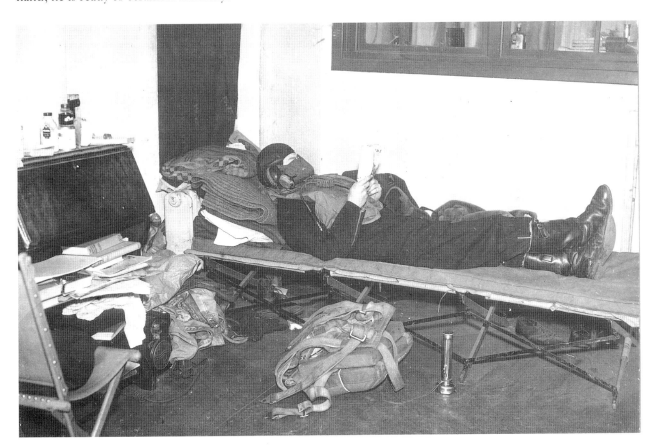

◆ The end of a bomber: the first aircraft to be shot down over Britain, this Heinkel III came to grief in Scotland, returning from a mission to bomb Royal Navy docks.

◆ Luftwaffe fighter crews wait for their orders, Germany 1940.

● Young RAF pilots gather round a Spitfire, Duxford Aerodrome.

● Fighter Command. In an operations room safely below ground, the WAAF (Women's Auxiliary Air Force) plotters position the aircraft according to constant information from detecting posts along the south coast of England. They are observed from the viewing gallery by senior officers.

➤ Bombing Thames installations at Purfleet.

THE BLITZ SEPTEMBER 1940–MAY 1941

With the discovery by the Luftwaffe that the RAF was very much their equal, the tactic switched from attacking air force bases and radar stations to one of terror bombing British cities, in an attempt to demoralise the population and to hit strategic targets such as dockyards, factories and workers' housing. Due to the success of the RAF against daytime raiders, the Luftwaffe switched to night-time bombing, making the bombers harder to spot. This also made the bombers' targets harder to hit, resulting in higher civilian casualties. With improvements to British air defences, the losses to the Luftwaffe increased, although the raids continued into spring 1941, including one raid on London on the night of 10/11 May which killed over 1,400 people. In the spring of 1941, Hitler's attention began to turn to the imminent Operation *Barbarossa* against the Soviet Union, and the Luftwaffe began transferring planes and personnel east. The immediate threat to Britain was over.

◆ Coventry Cathedral stands in ruins after a night-time visit from the bombers of the Luftwaffe, November 1940. The raid killed over 500 civilians and destroyed more than 15,000 buildings.

◗ A line of children board a ship to be evacuated to Australia, August 1940. Many would settle in Australia and never return to their homeland.

◄ A member of the LDV (Local Defence Volunteers), forerunner of the Home Guard, getting some rifle practice.

BATTLE OF THE ATLANTIC SEPTEMBER 1939–JUNE 1942

Although the period from September 1939 to April 1940 is often referred to as the 'Phoney War', at sea the situation was very different. The German Navy, the Kriegsmarine, had been building heavy capital ships, such as the *Graf Spee* and the *Deutschland*. With the outbreak of hostilities, these ships, already at sea, took up their stations in the South Atlantic, in an effort to starve the British into submission by destroying British merchant shipping. The *Graf Spee* in particular caused problems for the Royal Navy, until she was cornered off the River Plate in South America by a task force of British ships, including the heavy cruiser *Exeter*. In the ensuing battle, the *Graf Spee* was forced to seek shelter in neutral Montevideo, Uruguay, where she was scuttled in the harbour by her captain. However, the biggest danger to Allied shipping came from U-boats, the German submarines. Although few in number and limited in operational range at this stage, the submarines took a heavy toll of Allied merchantmen. The Royal Navy responded by re-introducing the convoy system of merchantmen guarded by warships, and this ensured that in the early stages of the war, at least, even the submarines came nowhere near sinking the 750,000 tonnes of shipping per month that the Kriegsmarine regarded as the minimum target in order to starve Britain into submission. With the fall of France in June 1940, the situation was to change again, however. Able to operate from bases in Occupied France, and using improved tactics such as long-range spotter aircraft and radio, the U-boat toll of shipping increased. With the loss of the battleship *Hood* in action against the *Bismarck*, the heaviest ship afloat, British morale took a further blow. It was somewhat restored with the eventual sinking of the *Bismarck* off the French coast by a combined British force. The overall situation by the summer of 1942, however, remained bleak.

◀ Grand Admiral of the German Kriegsmarine Erich Raeder (left) with his successor Karl Dönitz. Dönitz would also become leader of the Third Reich, after Hitler's suicide in May 1945.

➥ The *Graf Spee* under full steam. As a surface raider, the ship posed problems for the British Merchant Navy.

◀ The *Graf Spee* after being scuttled in Montevideo by Captain Langsdorff on 17 December 1939. Langsdorff later committed suicide.

The *Bismarck*, seen here off the coast of Norway from her fellow capital ship the *Prinz Eugen*.

HMS *Hood*, largest and most powerful ship in the British fleet at the outbreak of the Second World War.

◆ Another view of HMS *Hood*, seen here at anchor in Scapa Flow, the Royal Navy's main naval base for the North Atlantic.

◆ The *Bismarck* opens fire upon HMS *Hood*, in what would be the *Hood's* final battle. Although she was no match for the *Bismarck*, she fought bravely until an unlucky shot detonated her magazine.

▶ Men aboard a patrolling cutter of the US Coastguard sight sixteen men on a raft. Their ship has been torpedoed by a Nazi U-boat in the North Atlantic.

➡ The picture above shows the waves created by a German U-boat just before it surfaced and below the U-boat sinking after being bombed by Canadian aircraft, off the coast of Canada.

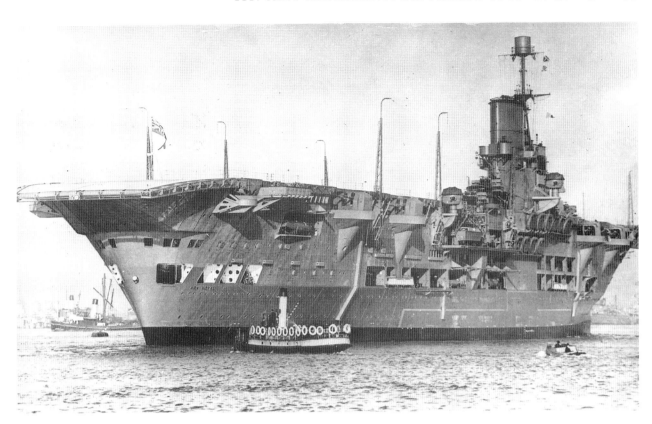

◆ HMS *Ark Royal*, seen here in more peaceful times, before the outbreak of war. Fairey Swordfish aircraft from the ship disabled the *Bismarck*, allowing the chasing British warships to catch up and sink her.

◆ German U-boats of the Atlantic fleet in dock, 1940.

4. East Africa June 1940–February 1941

On 10 June 1940, Italy declared war on Britain and France. Italy had gained little from the First World War under the Treaty of Versailles despite being on the winning side, and paying a high cost in lives. The resulting economic crisis brought about by the costs of the war combined with a resurgence in nationalistic feeling and bitterness over what the Italians perceived as the unjust terms of Versailles to provide support for Mussolini. The Fascist talk of 'seizing power' with their 1922 'March on Rome' is however absurdly self-dramatising, as with similar Nazi claims. The fact is that, as with Hitler in Germany, Mussolini was handed power by a conservative right-wing eager to manipulate the mass movements that both men had succeeded in building. As with Hitler, Mussolini proved more than capable of outmanoeuvring his political 'masters'.

In June 1940, eager to expand his incipient empire at the expense of the British, whom he believed would quickly be defeated by his stronger fellow dictator, Mussolini ordered the

invasion of the Sudan and Kenya, closely followed by British Somaliland and Egypt later the same year. The British response took a little while to come, but when it did it was devastating. In January 1941, a British force comprising 4th and 5th Indian Divisions attacked Italian strongholds in Eritrea, and a further British force under Lieutenant General Alan Cuningham captured Mogadishu before moving into Abyssinia from the south. By March 1941, with the exception of positions in the mountain stronghold of Amba Alagi, which held out until 3 May, all Italian possessions in East Africa were in British hands. Meanwhile in Egypt, which the Italians invaded in September 1940 under Marshal Rodolfo Graziani, British success was even more stunning. The Western Desert Force under Major General Richard O'Connor smashed the Italian front line west

▲ Italian field commander in Egypt, Marshal Rodolfo Graziani. The opportunistic Italian invasion of Egypt while Britain was engaged in France was destined to be a short one.

of Sidi Barrani, capturing over 38,000 troops: more than the 35,000 that O'Connor himself commanded. Taking advantage of the confusion in the Italian ranks, O'Connor pushed on into Libya. Despite some hard fighting around the Italian fortress of Bardia, O'Connor's 6th Australian Division had seized the vital port of Tobruk by 22 January 1941. Chasing the retreating Italians to the Gulf of Sirte, O'Connor managed to trap the entire Italian Tenth Army at Beda Fomm between the British 7th Armoured Division from the south, and the 6th Australian Division from the north. The Italians surrendered on 7 February, leaving O'Connor with 100,000 prisoners. The British counter-attack had lasted just two months, and advanced over 500 miles. It was a brilliant success, but the British failed to follow it up. Instead, many of O'Connor's more experienced units were transferred to Greece in the middle of February, to reinforce the Greek struggle against the Italians.

◆ Italian troops cross the border from Libya into Egypt.

◆ Italian soldiers surrendering during Major General Richard O'Connor's attack on the Italian fortress of Bardia, January 1941.

➤ Australian tanks of 6ᵗʰ Australian Division wait to enter Tobruk, January 1941.

⬆ Italian prisoners of war from the Bersaglieri Alpine regiment are questioned by British military police.

5. Greece and Yugoslavia April–May 1941

Following the unsuccessful Italian invasion of Greece, Mussolini requested help from Hitler. On 6 April, a massive German invasion of Greece and Yugoslavia, Operation *Marita*, was launched. Despite fierce Greek and Yugoslav resistance, bolstered by over 50,000 British troops, the German Panzers proved unstoppable. Athens was occupied, and around 40,000 British troops were evacuated under heavy fire from the Peloponnese by the end of April. *Blitzkrieg* had once again proved its tactical superiority. Around 30,000 British troops were evacuated to Crete, to reinforce the garrison there, under Major General Freyberg. Expecting a conventional, seaborne attack, the British were once again taken utterly by surprise, this time by a huge airborne assault, carried out by the paratroops of Major General Kurt Student. Crete fell on 29 May, after fierce resistance, and British troops had once again to be evacuated by the Royal Navy. The Battle of Crete was a success for the Germans, but they suffered huge casualties, and Hitler vowed never to undertake large-scale paratroop attacks again. The invasion of Crete remains the only airborne assault carried out at strategic level in the history of warfare.

➤ Greek troops defend their homeland against the German invasion in support of Mussolini, April 1942. The Greek resistance was valiant, but the German Panzer troops, as on so many other occasions during the war, proved unstoppable.

◀ General Kurt Student, creator of the German parachute division.

➥ General Student inspects his troops.

◀ German paratroops drop in on Crete.
Although the operation was a success, the cost
in men and equipment was so high that Hitler
vowed never to attempt another parachute
drop on this scale.

◀ Moving forward, cautiously. The German
invaders of Crete faced stubborn resistance, not
only from British and Empire troops under
Major General Freyberg, but also from the
inhabitants.

6. North Africa February 1941–June 1942

Alarmed by British success in the Western Desert, Hitler sent Rommel and the Afrika Korps to defend Libya. Arriving barely two weeks after the Battle of Beda Fomm, the Afrika Korps quickly pushed the overextended British back from El Agheila to Sollum in Egypt by June 1941, leaving Tobruk surrounded. The British had begun reinforcing Tobruk in May 1941, and the garrison held out, allowing Wavell to push forward and relieve the siege by December 1941, once again advancing as far as El Agheila, helped greatly by the activities of the Long Range Desert Group and the newly-formed Special Air Service (SAS) behind German lines. By 30 June 1942, however, the British had once again been forced back to beyond El Alamein. The situation in the Western Desert was complicated by the problem of extended supply lines over the vast distances involved, and has been compared to two boxers on the end of elastic ropes; as soon as one reaches the extent of his rope, he is forced to pull back. At the Battle of Gazala on 14 June 1942, however, Rommel seemed to have scored a key victory which, taken with the fall of Tobruk on 21 June 1942, meant that mid-1942 was the lowest point of the war for the Western Allies.

◀ 'The Desert Fox', General Erwin Rommel, perhaps the best tank tactician of the war.

◀ The swastika and the palm tree; the logo of the Afrika Korps.

➡ Members of the Long Range Desert Group returning from a three-month trip behind enemy lines. The LRDG operated in small groups, and specialised in surprise attacks and sabotage. They were later to be joined in this by the nascent Special Air Service, the SAS.

◆ The Fall of Tobruk. Allied troops are taken prisoner after holding out in the city for months without relief.

◗ The Fall of Tobruk. Rommel waits in his staff car to enter the city.

◆ The first German vehicle into Tobruk, 21 June 1942.

◀ Night firing by British 25-pounder during the Battle of Gazala, June 1942.

🖛 Knocked-out British Matilda tanks at Gazala.

🖙 British tank soldier emerges from his vehicle into the hands of the enemy during the Battle of Gazala.

⬆ Panzer IIIs pass through Russian village during Operation *Barbarossa*. For the initial assault on Russia the Germans had massed 17 Panzer and 11 motorised divisions.

7. The Eastern Front June 1941–August 1942

On 22 June 1941, Operation *Barbarossa*, the Nazi invasion of the Soviet Union, was launched. The nations of Europe were either neutral or occupied, Rommel was achieving success against the British in Egypt, and while there was some British success in the Middle East (Iraq, Syria and Iran would fall to the British by September 1941), the Atlantic convoys were struggling in the face of relentless submarine warfare. Hitler judged that the time had come for a lightning war against Russia, whose fighting ability he held in utter contempt, despite the warnings of his generals. In the initial stages, the German successes were stunning. With the practice of *Blitzkrieg* by then firmly established, the Wehrmacht, spearheaded by its elite Panzer divisions, had advanced over 400 miles in places, and taken a million prisoners by July, and was poised for an assault on Moscow. The advance on Moscow was halted, however, on Hitler's personal orders and much to the disgust of his generals in the field, in order to divert troops to consolidate the gains in the north and in the Ukraine. By the time the advance began again, it was too late; the Russian autumn had turned the roads to a quagmire, the infamous Russian *rasputiza*. Combined with overextended supply lines, and the Russian destruction of their own infrastructure, this delayed the German arrival at Moscow until the end of November. Soviet reinforcements, in particular that of 'General Winter', stalled the German offensive. The Soviets counter-attacked; the realities of making war on a country so vast, and with so many men at its disposal, were now becoming clear to the German generals, as they had to Napoleon before them. The Germans were pushed back along a 600-mile front, stretching from Leningrad in the north to the Sea of Azov in the south. Army Group South, however, now divided into Army Groups A and B, managed to eradicate a Soviet salient around Isyum, south of Kharkov, in May 1942, and the way lay open for a push to the Caucasus, Operation *Blue*. By August, Army Group A under List was just outside the Chechen city of Grozny. Army Group B under Weichs had reached Stalingrad. Hitler's Greater German Reich had reached its zenith.

◆ German infantry are well received as they roll into Lemberg in Poland, formerly in East Prussia.

◆ Motorised division on the way to Moscow.

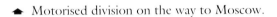

◆ A flight of the dreaded Junkers 87 dive-bombers, with Messerschmitt 109 escorts. Better known as the Stuka, the JU 87 was used extensively as a ground-support aircraft for the Panzers.

◆ A group of German soldiers pause for breath on a farm outside a Russian village. That they are regular army soldiers and not SS can be seen by their uniforms, and by the WH (*Wehrmacht–Heer* : Wehrmacht–Army) on the licence plates of the vehicles.

◀ German infantrymen advance through a burning Russian village during *Barbarossa*.

◆ Tired German infantry take a break on the way to Moscow. The strain of the pace of the German advance can be seen on their faces.

⬆ Captured in the opening days of *Barbarossa*, this group of Russian prisoners sit disconsolately together. The initial German attacks on the Soviet Union had yielded almost one million prisoners by the end of June 1941, many of whom would perish miserably in Germany working as slave labour.

➡ Russian T-34 tank, perhaps the best tank of the Second World War. With its sloping front and heavy side armour, broad tracks and heavy 76mm gun, the T-34 outclassed anything the Germans possessed in 1941.

◀ The Russian *rasputiza*, the autumn mud. Once the rains begin in Russia, most of the country becomes virtually impassable, as the Russians knew, and as the Germans, including this luckless motorcyclist, did not.

☞ Troops of the German Army Group Centre, accompanied by a STUG III (*Sturmgeschütz*, a self-propelled gun), reach an outer suburb of Moscow, December 1941. This would be as far as they would get.

◗ The execution of suspected partisan girl Zoya Kosmodemyanskaya, hanged by the Nazis. She fought with the hangman for time to call her last words, 'Farewell, Comrades! Stalin is with us, Stalin will come!'

(This is one of a series of four pictures found on a dead Nazi soldier in Smolensk.)

◖ German mortar crew prepare to open fire, Russia, Moscow campaign. By Christmas 1941, the advance units of Army Group Centre had been forced to retreat from Moscow, and take up winter quarters some distance away. Hitler was furious, and sacked a number of his officers, including General Guderian.

◆ Colonel General von Manstein, promoted to
Field Marshal after the fall of Sevastopol, July 1942.

◀ Oil wells burn in the Caucasus, fired by the retreating Russians to prevent their falling into German hands.

◆ Russian women look helplessly on as their village burns.

◆ Refuelling Stukas. Despite the Luftwaffe's much vaunted aerial supremacy over the Red Army Air Force, it would be unable to deliver anything like the amount of supplies needed by von Paulus's Sixth Army when it became encircled in the ruined city of Stalingrad during November 1942.

◆ Luftwaffe soldiers patrol Stalingrad, September 1942. Perhaps more than any other single battle, the four-month struggle for Stalingrad would prove a turning point of the war.

8. War in the Pacific 7 December 1941–May 1942

On 7 December 1941 the American Pacific naval base at Pearl Harbor was attacked by the Japanese fleet. In what President Roosevelt would later refer to as a 'day that would live in infamy', there was no warning given, and no prior declaration of war. At around 8.00 a.m. the first wave of carrier-based Japanese fighter-bombers began the attack on the base, followed at around 8.30 by a second wave. Although this second wave lost some aircraft, the final outcome was a huge US loss, including five out of eight battleships destroyed and the other three damaged. In all, the US lost 18 ships, and a total of around 350 out of 400 aircraft. The victory was less successful than it appeared, however. The US carrier fleet, the main target of the attack, was safely out to sea when the attack occurred, and survived untouched. More importantly, with Hitler's declaration of war on the US on 11 December, out of loyalty to his Japanese ally, the Second World War truly became a world war.

At the same time as the Japanese navy was attacking Pearl Harbor, its armies began the attack on Malaya and Hong Kong. The sinking of the British battleships *Prince of Wales* and *Repulse*

➥ The USS *West Virginia* and USS *Tennessee* are hit during the surprise Japanese attack on the US naval base at Pearl Harbor, 7 December 1941. This attack brought the United States into the war.

by the Japanese navy was a major blow to British prestige, as was the speed of the Japanese advance. Hong Kong surrendered on Christmas Day, 1941; the poorly-defended outpost of Singapore held out until 15 February 1942. Guam and Wake Island, US airbases in the Marianas were captured in the same month, and the Japanese also invaded the Philippines. The US troops on the Philippines under General Douglas MacArthur were forced to retreat before the Japanese onslaught, eventually holing up in the Bataan Peninsula, to the west of the Philippine capital of Manila. President Roosevelt, realising that the trapped men could not hold out, and could not be evacuated, ordered General MacArthur to leave. The trapped US troops surrendered on 9 April, and were marched to distant prisoner of war camps, under conditions that resulted in the death of many of the 78,000 US and Filipino troops. This quickly became known as the 'Bataan Death March', and would set the tone for much of the fighting in the Pacific that was to come. The Dutch East Indies, modern-day Indonesia, were taken by the Japanese during March 1942, and the US island fortress of Corregidor in Manila Bay surrendered on 6 May. The Japanese advance through British-held Burma was equally swift: it also had fallen by May 1942. The British Burma Army, despite support from the Chinese Fifth Army under the leadership of US General Joseph Stilwell, was forced into the longest retreat in its history, almost 1,000 miles, to the Indian border. Under Major General William Slim, however, the retreat was made in good order, and the British regrouped around Kohima and Imphal, where they dug in and prepared to ride out the Japanese storm.

◀ A remarkable image of the powder magazine of the US destroyer *Shaw* exploding at the exact moment this photo is taken.

▶ Headline in the *Los Angeles Times*, reporting the US and British declaration of war on Japan following the attacks on Pearl Harbor.

EXTRA

IT'S WAR!

Hostilities Declared by Japanese; 350 Reported Killed in Hawaii Raid

U.S. Battleships Hit; 7 Die in Honolulu

NEW YORK, Dec. 7. (A.P.)—Three hundred and fifty men were killed by a direct bomb hit on Hickam Field an N.B.C. observer reported tonight from Honolulu.

In addition to these casualties from an air raid by planes which the observer identified as Japanese, he said three United States ships, including the battleship Oklahoma, were attacked in Pearl Harbor.

Several of the attacking planes, which came from the south, were shot down, he said.

HONOLULU, Dec. 7. (A.P.)—Japanese bombs killed at least seven persons and injured many others, three seriously, in a surprise morning aerial attack on Honolulu today.

Army officials announced that two Japanese planes had been shot down in the Honolulu area.

The dead included three Caucasians, two Japanese and a 10-year-old Portuguese girl.

Several fires were started in the city area, but all were immediately controlled.

Governor Joseph B. Poindexter proclaimed M-Day emergency defense measures immediately in effect. He appointed Eduard Doty in charge of the Major Disaster Council.

The M-Day proclamation establishes civilian-military control of traffic and roads, and permits the Governor to issue food ration regulations.

First reports said that 10 or more persons were injured when enemy planes sprayed bullets on the streets of Wahiawa, a town of about 3000 population, about 20 miles northwest of Honolulu.

This report indicated the aerial attack was aimed at points on the island of Oahu other than Honolulu and the heavily fortified Pearl Harbor naval base.

The attack ended at around 9:25 a.m., (11:55 a.m. P.S.T.) lasting for ap-

Turn to Page B, Column 7

LATE WAR BULLETINS

SHANGHAI, Dec. 8 (Monday.) (A.P.)—The Japanese have sunk the British gunboat Petrel as it lay off the International Settlement waterfront.

HONOLULU, Dec. 7. (U.P.) — Parachute troops were sighted off Pearl Harbor today.

TOKYO, Dec. 8 (Monday.) (A.P.)—An emergency session of the Japanese Cabinet was held at Premier Tojo's official residence at 7 a.m. today (2 p.m. Sunday, P.S.T.)

NEW YORK, Dec. 7. (U.P.)—The U.S.S. Oklahoma, a battleship, was set afire in today's air attack on Pearl Harbor, an N.B.C. broadcast from Honolulu said.

WASHINGTON, Dec. 7. (A.P.)—The Navy Department announced tonight that a censorship had been placed on all outgoing cablegrams and radio messages from the United States and its outlying possessions.

LONDON, Dec. 7. (AP)—The House of Commons was summoned tonight for a session tomorrow.

The House of Lords also was called.

An announcement from Prime Minister

Turn to Page B, Column 3

Air Guards, Attention!

To chief observers: All observation posts:
A.W.S. (Aircraft Warning Service) You are directed to activate your observation posts immediately and to see that the post is fully manned at all times.

By order Brig. Gen. William O. Ryan, Commander, Ft. Interceptor Command.

Air Bombs Rained on Pacific Bases

WASHINGTON, Dec. 7. (A.P.)—The White House announced early tonight that the Navy had advised the President that Japan has attacked the island of Guam.

WASHINGTON, Dec. 7. (A.P.)—Japan declared war upon the United States today. An electrified nation immediately united for a terrific struggle ahead. President Roosevelt was expected to ask Congress for a declaration of war tomorrow.

During the day, Japanese planes bombed Manila, Honolulu, Pearl Harbor, and Hickam Field, Hawaii, without warning. In a broadcast from Honolulu, some 350 soldiers were reported dead at Hickam Field, with numerous casualties at the other points of attack. (The attack on Manila was announced by the White House. The Associated Press correspondent there reported at 1:25 p.m. (P.S.T.) that Manila was quiet.) President Roosevelt said he hoped the report of the bombing of the Philippine capital "at least is erroneous."

Then, the Tokyo government announced that Japan had entered a state of war with the United States and Great Britain as of 6 a.m., tomorrow (1 p.m. P.S.T. Sunday.)

But President Roosevelt hardly waited for the Japanese declaration. As soon as he heard of the bombing he ordered the Army and Navy to carry out previously prepared and highly secret plans for the defense of the country.

Army airmen engaged Japanese fighting planes over Honolulu. In the city below them, the White House said, a heavy loss of life had been inflicted, together with extensive damage to property.

At the same time, the Chief Executive called his Cabinet into extraordinary session for 8:30 p.m., and invited Congressional leaders to join the group a half-hour later.

Prior to this meeting, Mr. Roosevelt began the draft of a special message to Congress and if the general sentiment in official Washington quarters was any indication, Japan's declaration of war would be met in like terms by the Commander-in-Chief.

From a high Congressional source, it was learned that the President mentioned the possibility of a joint session of Congress tomorrow. This naturally led to speculation that the Chief Executive would address it and ask in person, as did Woodrow Wilson in 1917, that it declare war.

Turn to Page B, Column 1

➤ The Japanese battleship *Yamato* is fitted out at Kure in Japan, prior to the Japanese attack on Pearl Harbor.

➤ Fleet of Japanese Zeros assembled at the start of the war in the Pacific.

◀ Japanese Prime Minister Hideki Tojo. A fervent nationalist, Tojo was the architect of Japanese military strategy during World War Two, and personally ordered the surprise attack on Pearl Harbor. A competent strategist, Tojo nevertheless overestimated the effect the Japanese attacks would have on the Allies, and vastly underestimated the Allied will to fight.

Compelled to resign after the loss of the Mariana Islands in 1944, he was arrested by the US after the Japanese surrender. Tried as a war criminal, he was convicted and hanged on 23 December 1948.

➡ Japanese infantry on the march in Malaya, 1942.

➤ Survivors scramble to safety from the broken British battleship *Prince of Wales*, sunk after being hit by Japanese bombers on 10 December 1941. The British battlecruiser *Repulse* was also destroyed in the same attack.

◆ Mounted Japanese troops enter Hong Kong, led by Lieutenant General Sakai and Vice Admiral Niimi, Christmas Day 1941.

◆ British weapon carriers lie abandoned as the Japanese army marches past on its way into Singapore. Despite numerical superiority, the Singapore garrison was poorly deployed, with British commanders unaware of the Japanese ability to fight through jungle.

◀ Victorious Japanese troops march past the Singapore General Post Office, after the surrender of the British garrison, 15 February 1942.

➡ General Percival, commander of the British garrison in Singapore, surrenders to the Japanese.

◀ Japanese marines enter a town in the Philippines after heavy fighting.

US officers are escorted to the Japanese command during the surrender of the Philippines, having held out in the Bataan Peninsula for three months. Their commander, General Douglas MacArthur had earlier been ordered by President Roosevelt to leave the Philippines. His final words to his troops were 'I shall return'.

Japanese troops in the Philippines, January 1942, following the US retreat to the Bataan Peninsula, which the Japanese attacked on 9 January.

US prisoners after the surrender of the Philippines to the Japanese.

Japanese troops attack the oilfields at Yenangyaung in Burma, April 1942. The British Burma Corps would make a fighting retreat, but by May Burma was effectively in Japanese hands.

Triumphant Japanese soldiers celebrate the fall of Burma, May 1942.

The Japanese Emperor Hirohito inspects his troops.

SITUATION ASSESSMENT: SUMMER 1942

THE SUMMER OF 1942 are the darkest days of the war for the Allies. The staggeringly successful Japanese attacks from Pearl Harbor in December 1941 to the fall of Burma in May, 1942, have utterly stunned the Allies. The effectiveness of the Japanese military machine has shocked the world, and the Japanese Emperor looks ideally positioned actually to build himself an empire. The scale of these defeats, followed as they are by disaster in North Africa with the fall of Tobruk in June, and the beginning of the German siege of Stalingrad in August gives a bleak outlook for the direction of the war. The havoc being wreaked on Britain's vital Atlantic convoys by Dönitz's Wolf Packs casts a grave doubt on her ability even to continue fighting, while the US has barely entered the war, has lost a significant proportion of its Pacific Fleet, and possesses only a small and untried army.

Success from this point will be due to improved weapons and tactics, the genius of individual commanders, and not least of all, US industrial muscle.

IV: HALTING THE AXIS: JUNE 1942–AUGUST 1943

1. North Africa July 1942–May 1943

THE FIRST HALT to the seemingly inexorable advances being made by the Axis powers came at the First Battle of El Alamein in July 1942. The British, having retreated in good order after the Battle of Gazala, were well dug in; Rommel and his Afrika Korps had reached the end of their chain of supplies and were stretched to breaking point. Although the battle was not entirely a success for the British, the advancing Rommel had at least been halted. After the battle, the commander of the British Eighth Army was replaced by General Sir Bernard Montgomery, a tactician of a different order from his predecessor. After fighting Rommel off in the defensive battle of Alam Halfa, Montgomery went over to the attack in October, inflicting a heavy defeat on the Afrika Korps at the Second Battle of El Alamein, an armoured push known as Operation *Supercharge*. Although expensive in terms of men and equipment – the battle cost

➥ General Sir Bernard Montgomery replaced General Sir Claude Auchinleck as commander of Eighth Army in Egypt. Auchinleck's original replacement, Lieutenant General William Gott, was killed in August 1942.

the British 13,000 casualties and over 200 tanks – it had Rommel on the run. Winston Churchill would later say of the battle 'before Alamein we never had a victory. After Alamein, we never had a defeat'. The Operation *Torch* landings in French North Africa meant that the Germans were caught between the US and the rapidly advancing British Eighth Army, who recaptured Tobruk on 13 November. Although the Americans suffered a heavy defeat at the Kasserine Pass in mid-February 1943, the arrival of new tanks and men meant the end for Rommel and his Afrika Korps: acting commander General Arnim surrendered on 12 May 1943. The Allied campaign in North Africa had reached a successful conclusion. Now came Italy.

🔺 German Panzer III, destroyed near Tel-el-Eissa Station during the Battle of Alam Halfa, August 1942. The battle was the first clear British success against the Afrika Korps.

🔺 Italian troops running for cover as British bombs rain down during an RAF attack on Axis positions, during the Second Battle of El Alamein.

British infantry charge an enemy position amidst the smoke and confusion of battle, Second Alamein.

Hande hoch! German Panzer crew surrenders to British infantryman, Second Alamein.

◆ British Honey tank passes a knocked out German Panzer III. The figure in the foreground is a British artillery officer taking advantage of the cover to establish a forward listening post.

◆ Two Allied soldiers cautiously observe the burning wreckage of two German armoured vehicles after Rommel's Afrika Korps retreat in the North African desert.

☞ Hit by the 105mm howitzer of a US tank destroyer (left) in North Africa, a heavy German tank is destroyed by flames. US 'tank busters' of this type have played an important role in the advance of the British Eighth Army against Rommel's forces.

☞ Lieutenant General Dwight Eisenhower (left), and Major General Mark Clark negotiate the US Operation *Torch* landings in French Morocco with French Admiral Darlan (centre), 13 November 1942. The landings would trap Rommel's Afrika Korps between US forces and the British Eighth Army, advancing rapidly through Libya.

◗ Major General George S. 'Blood and Guts' Patton, commander of US troops in North Africa. Patton had been a tank commander since the First World War, and played a vital role in the training of US tank troops.

◗ US tank soldiers clean out the barrel of their Grant tank, after the capture of the village of Medjez-el-Bab.

 US soldier with slung Tommy gun gazes at the dead face of the enemy, Tunisia, 1943.

◗ Despondent Afrika Korps soldier taken prisoner in French North Africa, April 1943.

2. Bombing Germany 1942–1945

The strategy for bombing the German homeland began in confusion, with no one very sure of which targets they should be aiming at. This, coupled with ineffective bombers and poor navigational abilities led to a very limited success in the initial stages of the bombing campaign. The campaign was suspended in November 1941 after 37 aircraft were lost in one night over

Germany. In February 1942, Arthur 'Bomber' Harris was appointed as Commander-in-Chief, Bomber Command. Harris realised that the key to success was to increase the number of bombers on missions, swamping the German air defences and outnumbering the night fighters. With the limited accuracy of the bombers in mind, Harris issued his Area Bombing Directive of 14 February 1942, designating German cities as targets. This move was to change the whole bombing strategy. Bomber production doubled between 1940 and 1942, and the amount of bombs dropped by the RAF increased from 13,000 tonnes to 45,000 tonnes over the same period.

On 30 May 1942, the first 1,000-bomber raid was launched on Cologne, possibly in retaliation for the 1940 German raid on Coventry. It left the city devastated; only the cathedral in the centre was left standing.

From August 1942, the US became involved, and the first joint operation took place in July 1943. On the night of 16/17 May, 617 Squadron of the RAF carried out the 'Dambusters Raid' on the Moehne, Sorpe and Eder dams in the Cologne–Kassell area, a raid which had far more effect on the German war machine than the bombing of cities. As with the British during the Blitz, the bombing of civilians simply stiffened their will to resist.

The worst bombing of Hamburg on the night of 28/29 July created a firestorm in which an estimated 40,000 people died. The bombing of civilians was never a concept which the British people were eager to acknowledge, and after the war, Harris was refused a decoration, and the bomber crews were denied a campaign medal of their own. This overlooks the fact that during the years 1940–1943, Bomber Command was the only branch of the services able to strike directly at Reich territory, and that 55,000 bomber crew members gave their lives to maintain the pressure on the Third Reich. It was a shabby way to treat brave men.

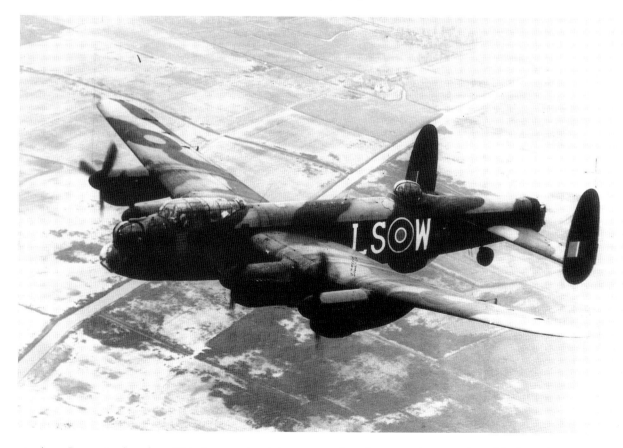

⬥ Avro Lancaster bomber. This four-engined, long-range bomber came into service with the RAF in 1942, and proved to be one of the most effective bombers of the war.

↟ 12,000lb bomb is loaded onto a Lancaster by RAF ground personnel.

↟ The castle at Nuremberg, southern Germany, after an Allied air attack. The city of Nuremberg would become the site of the war crimes trials after the war.

↞ The twin spires of Cologne cathedral stand defiantly amidst the rubble of an air attack.

↞ The Moehne Dam in Germany, pictured before the famous 'Dambusters' raid by 617 Squadron on the night of 16/17 May 1943. In all, 19 aircraft took part in the raids on three dams across Germany.

◗ Boeing B-17 'Flying Fortresses' of the US Army Air Force, en route to attack Merkwiller in Germany, 3 August 1943.

☛ Flying Fortresses on a night raid over Bremen, Germany. The switch by the USAAF from daytime to night-time raids cut down on casualties amongst bomber crews.

▶ Under the bombs; a Hamburg church stands in ruins.

➤ The bodies of civilians, including that of a small girl, lie strewn across the streets of their city. Hamburg, along with Dresden would suffer horrific firestorms as a result of heavy bombing in the Second World War. The practice of deliberately targeting civilians has never been called more into question than after the July 1943 raids on Hamburg which created a firestorm that left 40,000 people dead.

3. Battle of the Atlantic June 1942–August 1943

The introduction of the escorted convoy system off the US coast saw a dramatic fall in losses to merchantmen. The focus of U-boats was therefore switched by Dönitz back to the North Atlantic, using the 'Wolf Pack' system of waves of U-boat attacks on the same convoy. By March 1943, the situation was so bleak there was a suggestion that Britain could no longer maintain the war effort.

That Britain was in fact able to continue was due to five main factors:

1. The introduction of long-range aircraft such as the Shorts Sunderland and the B-24 Liberator, equipped with better radar, Leigh searchlights, machine guns and depth charges, to provide air cover for convoys, and to attack U-boats;
2. Increased use of escort carriers;
3. The enormous shipbuilding efforts of the US, turning out a merchant ship, or 'Liberty ship' as they became known, in a matter of days;
4. The introduction of 'River' class frigates, fast, dedicated submarine hunter-killers;
5. The cracking of the German Enigma code using Ultra, a cryptography system based at Bletchley Park in England.

Although the introduction in 1944 of the *schnorkel* type submarines which could stay submerged for far longer periods threatened the Allies until the end of the war, by 1943, the Germans had privately conceded defeat in the Battle of the Atlantic.

◀ The huge German battleship *Tirpitz*, sister ship of the *Bismarck*, seen here off Norway in the early stages of the war. At 50,000 tonnes, *Tirpitz* was one of the heaviest battleships of the war.

◆ *Tirpitz* seen here at her moorings in Narvik–Bogen Fjord, Norway, July 1942. The anti-submarine nets can clearly be seen to either side of the ship. Despite numerous attacks on the *Tirpitz* by both sea and air, she was not sunk until 12 November 1944, by Lancasters from 9 and 617 'Dambusters' squadrons of the Royal Air Force.

▶ The US merchant ship *Robert E. Peary* is launched, four days and fifteen hours after its keel was laid, a world record. The turnaround time for the US 'Liberty' ships was greatly aided by the use of prefabricated parts.

↟ Another Allied weapon against the Kriegsmarine, the convoy system. Here, a Royal Navy vessel (foreground, flying the White Ensign) escorts a group of merchantmen across the Atlantic.

↟ U-boat ace Captain Otto Kretschmer, photographed shortly after receiving the Oak Leaves to his Knight's Cross from Hitler, 4 November 1940. Although captured by the British in March 1941, he had sunk 47 ships, a total loss of 275,000 tonnes.

↟ Alan Turing. A Cambridge-trained mathematician, Alan Turing was largely responsible for the cracking of the German Enigma naval code, allowing the Royal Navy to track the movements of the German U-boats.

4. Eastern Front August 1942–July 1943

The battle for Stalingrad began in August 1942 as advanced units of Army Group South reached the city, and lasted until January 1943, when the demoralised and starving remnants of Paulus's Sixth Army surrendered. Both sides were prepared to make huge sacrifices for the city which bore the name of the Soviet leader. Marshal Chuikov mounted a spirited defence of Stalingrad as Russian reserves were poured in. Learning from the German *Kesselschlacht* tactic, they surrounded Stalingrad, and while the Soviets were able to obtain supplies of food, arms and men from across the Volga, the Germans were cut off, with the Luftwaffe consistently unable to provide anywhere near the estimated 300 tonnes of supplies needed daily by the men in Stalingrad. Faced with an impossible situation, the survivors of Sixth Army surrendered on 31 January. Over 90,000 were taken prisoner; few were ever seen again. The Russians continued to push the exhausted Germans back in a massive offensive which took them to Kharkov by February. The Germans under the indomitable Field Marshal Manstein retook Kharkov in some of the heaviest fighting of the war. In July 1943, however, the German attempt to eliminate the Kursk salient was heavily defeated in the largest tank battle in history outside the village of Prokhorovka, involving some 8,000 tanks altogether. The Germans suffered huge losses of men and equipment that could not be replaced.

◆ German infantry of Army Group South advance through Kharkov on the way to the Crimea and Stalingrad. The city would change hands more than once during the campaign.

◗ German infantry move into Stalingrad, August 1942.

➡ Sixth Army infantry, supported by a STUG (*Sturmgeschütz*, a self-propelled gun) move cautiously forward during the fighting for Stalingrad.

◗ Women digging near damaged railway tracks, Stalingrad 1942.

◆ Taking careful aim, this Wehrmacht soldier waits for the enemy, Stalingad, October 1942. The street fighting for the city was brutal and merciless in the extreme.

◆ Commanders: the commander of the doomed German Sixth Army, General von Paulus, inspects the position, while his opponent, Marshal Vasili Chuikov (right) enjoys a cigar while examining his map. Chuikov's grim defence of Stalingrad provided the Red Army with ample time to regroup and encircle the Germans within the city.

← Russian counter-attack at Stalingrad. The ferocity of the fighting is evident from the destruction all around them.

◀ German soldiers retreat from the Ukraine, February 1943, after the Russian capture of Stalingrad earlier in the year.

◀ Kharkov, March 1943; German troops engage the enemy.

➡ The Battle for Kharkov; German soldiers lie dead behind a burnt-out Russian tank.

▶ German troops evacuate a house destroyed by Russian artillery fire, Kharkov, spring 1943.

◗ Colonel General Walther Model, Hitler's 'fireman' (centre), famed for his ability to rescue impossible situations. The situation in Russia in 1943 was to prove beyond even his formidable abilities, however.

5. The Pacific April 1942–August 1943

In April 1942 bombers from the USS *Hornet* hit Tokyo, demonstrating to the Japanese their vulnerability. The Japanese, meanwhile, concentrated on attacking the USS Pacific Fleet under Nimitz.

In the Battle of the Coral Sea in May 1942, the Japanese advance on New Guinea was halted, with the loss of Japanese carrier *Shoho* and US carrier *Lexington*.

The Battle of Midway took place in June 1942, and marked the point where the US began to go over to the offensive. The Japanese were defeated by the US aircraft carrier force comprising *Hornet, Enterprise* and *Yorktown*, losing four carriers and over 300 aircraft that they could not replace. Although the US suffered the loss of the carrier *Yorktown* and around 100 aircraft, replacing them was not a problem, once the massive US industrial capacity was geared up to war production. After Midway, the US was always on the attack.

The 1st US Marine Division took the island stronghold of Guadalcanal in a surprise attack in August 1942, and, reinforced by the 7th Marines, held out against huge Japanese attacks until February 1943. The tactical significance of the island was high; the effect of the Marines' stubborn defence on Allied morale was incalculable, showing as it did that the feared Japanese could be taken on and beaten.

A Japanese attack on New Guinea in July 1942 was repulsed by US and Australian forces, and the Japanese strongholds of Buna and Gona had fallen by January 1943.

New Georgia was taken by August 1943, and the springboard for the US island-hopping campaign was in place.

◗ Devastator torpedo-bombers prepare to take off from the USS *Enterprise* off Midway, June 1942.

Meanwhile the British Burma Corps had regrouped in India, across the border from Burma, and Wingate's Chindits, while not strategically significant, were busy demonstrating that the Japanese could be taken on in jungle warfare and defeated.

The British Fourteenth Army was formed under General William Slim, and prepared for a counter-offensive in Burma.

◀ Japanese battleship *Hiryu*, Midway June 1942. The aircraft that destroyed the USS *Yorktown* on 5 June were launched from the *Hiryu*, but she was herself sunk later the same day.

➡ USS *Yorktown* in action at the Battle of Midway in the Pacific, 4 June 1942.

▶ The view from the deck of the *Yorktown* after being hit by Japanese bombers. She sank later the same day.

◆ US Marines pour onto the beach of Guadalcanal in the Solomon Islands, early on 7 August 1942. The Marines were able to catch the Japanese unawares, and by the next day had secured the vital airfield. The fighting on Guadalcanal would last until February 1943, however, as the Japanese attempted desperately to retake the island.

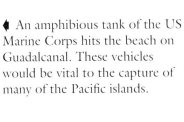

An amphibious tank of the US Marine Corps hits the beach on Guadalcanal. These vehicles would be vital to the capture of many of the Pacific islands.

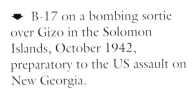

B-17 on a bombing sortie over Gizo in the Solomon Islands, October 1942, preparatory to the US assault on New Georgia.

British Army General Orde Wingate in discussion with a brigadier, Burma, 1942. Orde Wingate's Chindits (the name is taken from the *chinthe*, the mythical lion that guards Buddhist temples) hit the Japanese behind their lines, and showed the British that it was possible to take on the Japanese successfully.

SECTION IV: THE ALLIES TAKE THE OFFENSIVE: JULY 1943–AUGUST 1945

1. Southern Europe July 1943–May 1945

The invasion of Sicily from North Africa lasted 38 days and cost over 30,000 casualties, but the island was secured by 17 August, and provided a springboard for the invasion of the Italian mainland on 1 September 1943. The Italian surrender came days later, on 3 September 1943, with the new provisional Italian government switching sides to join the Allies. The Germans reacted in decisive fashion to this desertion by an ally, placing Italy under martial law, and reinforcing the Panzer Division *Herman Göring* with Vietinghoff's Tenth Army. The fighting in Italy was some of the heaviest of the war, particularly around Cassino, where the monastery held out against French, US, New Zealand, Indian and British troops, before the Polish Corps finally occupied it, although only after Kesselring had completed a tactical German withdrawal. The 45,000 Allied casualties reminded some observers of the First World War, while some Germans described conditions as 'worse than Stalingrad'. By December 1944, however, Allied troops had smashed through the German defences of the Gothic Line, and taken up positions north of Ravenna in the east and Pisa in the west.

⬥ Lieutenant General Mark Clark, commander of the US Fifth Army, comprising the US VI Corps and the British X Corps which landed at Salerno in September 1943. Opposed by General Vietinghoff's Tenth Army, they found the going tough, but had broken out of their bridgeheads by the end of September.

◗ US Sherman tanks come ashore at Anzio, Italy, January 1944. Italy had surrendered and changed sides on 3 September 1943; the Germans quickly disarmed the Italian Army and took over the defence of Italy.

➤ Mussolini, Germany July 1944. Taken prisoner on the surrender of Italy in September 1943, Mussolini was the subject of a daring German rescue led by super-commando Major Otto Skorzeny. He was allowed by the Germans to set up a Fascist mini-republic in the north of Italy, however even Hitler's unusual patience with his bungling ally was by this time wearing thin, and he was strictly controlled by the German commander on the spot.

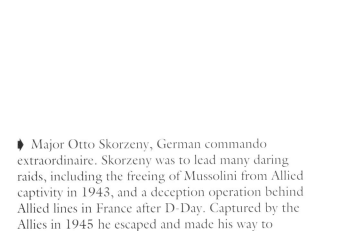

◗ Major Otto Skorzeny, German commando extraordinaire. Skorzeny was to lead many daring raids, including the freeing of Mussolini from Allied captivity in 1943, and a deception operation behind Allied lines in France after D-Day. Captured by the Allies in 1945 he escaped and made his way to Argentina, like so many other Nazis, where he became bodyguard to Eva Peron. Never recaptured, he died in bed in 1975.

◆ German soldier with MP40 sub-machine gun during the fighting for the town of Monte Cassino, May 1944.

◆ The historic town and monastery of Monte Cassino, pounded by artillery until it resembles a series of caves in the hillside.

← Aftermath; British troops advance through the ruins of the once-beautiful town on Cassino.

← The monastery perched on the top of Cassino hill in flames.

◆ End of a dictator: Mussolini and his mistress Clarette Petacci dangle in the marketplace of Milan, after their execution by Italian partisans, 28 April 1945.

2. The Eastern Front August 1943–May 1945

The Russians exploited the gains made after the Battle of Kursk, and retook Kharkov, for the second time, on 23 August 1943. The Soviets had used the time to build up huge reserves, and were boosted by the increasing supply of American equipment that now began to arrive as the Allies gained the upper hand in the Atlantic. By December 1943, they had pushed the Germans back across the Dnieper in most places, and trapped around 120,000 German and Romanian troops in the Crimean Peninsula. The Red Army also attacked along an immense front to the north, raising the siege of Leningrad in January. Due to Hitler's 'standfast' order to the troops, many German units were needlessly sacrificed to the seemingly unstoppable Red Army. Operation *Bagration*, launched in June 1944, saw the Soviets reach the River Vistula in Poland, where they halted and watched as the Germans destroyed Warsaw in a two-month orgy of revenge, using 'special' troops such as the Dirlewanger Brigade, under the command of a convicted sex criminal, Oskar Dirlewanger.

◆ Soviet gun crew advance with their 7.62mm cannon.

By the end of 1944, however, the Russian advance on the homeland of the Third Reich was taking place along a huge front, reaching from the Baltic in the north to the southern states of Eastern Europe.

➤ A stream of German prisoners begins the long, weary journey into captivity, under the curses of watching locals. Few of the soldiers will see Germany again.

➤ German infantrymen cautiously approach a Soviet Josef Stalin tank, somewhere on the Eastern Front. Only the German Tiger tank could hope to come out best of an encounter with one of these Soviet behemoths.

☛ German troops trail wearily in the wake of a Tiger tank during the retreat from the Eastern Front, March 1944.

☛ Destruction in Warsaw: knowing the war in the East, at least, was lost, the SS under the leadership of SS-General Erich von dem Bach-Zelewski nevertheless unleashed a reign of hell upon the unfortunate inhabitants of Warsaw. The advancing Russians halted on the far bank of the Vistula under Stalin's orders, allowing the Polish Home Army under General Bor-Komorowski to be destroyed.

☛ Frozen: the frost-rimed faces of these exhausted German soldiers tell the tale of the misery of the Eastern Front, March 1944.

Polish Home Army officers in German captivity after the defeat of the two-month long uprising in Warsaw, October 1944.

☛ Polish hostages hanged during the Warsaw uprising by the ever-busy SS, never unduly concerned with the status of civilians.

☛ Estonian SS volunteers burn a 'Bolshevik' village, Estonia, 1944. The realisation that the war was lost and that they had picked the wrong side made many locally-recruited SS volunteers behave with particular savagery.

☛ Reprisals: a crowd outside the Russian village of Orlov watches as partisans execute a man found guilty of collaborating with the Germans.

◆ Red Army Marshal Georgi Zhukov.

◆ Marshal Ivan Koniev.

▶ Soviet tanks in Berlin, May 1945. The fighting for the city would last for some weeks, but the end was never in doubt.

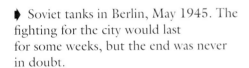

◀ T-34 tanks of the Red Army rolls down the highway to Berlin, accompanied by infantry.

▲ The final act: Soviet troops outside the Reichstag prior to hoisting the hammer and sickle above the burnt-out German parliament building. The Reichstag, which had housed the German parliament that did so little to curb Hitler's megalomaniac excesses, would ironically become the symbol of his defeat.

3. Western Europe June 1944–May 1945

Bulgaria and Romania changed sides in late 1944, and took part with Soviet troops in attacks on Albania, Hungary and Yugoslavia, where they were aided by Marshal Tito's Partisans. The British replaced withdrawing German troops in Greece, only to be caught up in a vicious civil war, destined to last well beyond August 1945.

On 6 June, 1944, the largest seaborne invasion in history was put into operation: D-Day, the liberation of Occupied Europe. By midnight on 6 June, 150,000 Allied soldiers had fought their way across the five invasion beaches, and had begun the long slog through Normandy on their way to Germany. Although the Germans put up stiff resistance, Allied air superiority meant that by September 1944 the German border with France had been reached, with Paris being liberated in August. The Allies suffered a setback at Arnhem in September, when airborne units were cut off attempting to capture a bridge across the Rhine: 'a bridge too far'. Nevertheless, the momentum had become unstoppable. In December 1944 the Germans mounted one final, desperate assault through the Ardennes Forest – the Battle of the Bulge – scene of stunning victories in 1940. The assault won ground, but failed to hold it. Units of the 101st US Airborne Division raced to Bastogne, and held out against the Panzer *Lehr* Division, creating an effective roadblock. When requested to surrender, US commanding officer Brigadier General Anthony McAuliffe famously replied, 'Nuts!' By January the attack was over, and the last German armour had been thrown away for nothing.

The Rhine was crossed in March 1945, and the Allies began to push deep into the German heartland, the Americans in the centre and south, the British in the north. The liberation of the concentration – not extermination – camps on German soil revealed the extent of Nazi atrocities. On 25 April 1945, Allied troops joined up with their Soviet counterparts on the Elbe at Torgau, and Germany was effectively cut in two. With the Red Army in Berlin under Zhukov and Koniev closing in on the Chancellery itself, Hitler committed suicide on 30 April 1945.

On 2 May 1945 the last commander of Berlin, General Karl Weidling, surrendered the city to the Soviets, and on 7 May 1945, the last commander of the Third Reich, Admiral Karl Dönitz and OKW Chief General Alfred Jodl surrendered unconditionally to the Allies. Europe's long night was over.

◆ British naval personnel captured after the commando raid on St Nazaire, France, 26 March 1942. Although casualties were high, the raid was at least successful, destroying the only dry dock close to the Alantic capable of accommodating a battleship.

▲ A burnt-out landing craft and abandoned Churchill tanks show where the over-ambitious raid on Dieppe came to grief on 19 August 1942. Although a failure in itself, the raid provided valuable lessons for the conduct of D-Day less than two years later.

◀ General Dwight D. Eisenhower, Allied Supreme Commander on D-Day, 6 June 1944.

▼ Allied LCIs (Landing Craft Infantry) cross the Channel in the early hours of 6 June.

➤ US LCIs land troops on Omaha Beach during the D-Day landings. The troops on Omaha Beach encountered the German 352nd Infantry Division, fresh from the Eastern Front, and suffered heavy casualties. It was only when the Royal Navy destroyers nearby realised the situation and moved in with fire support, coming in so close to shore that they were hit by rifle fire, that the beach was finally secured.

US troops head for Omaha Beach.

Survivors of a sunken LCI are hauled ashore by their buddies on the beach.

◆ Bloodied but unbowed, a young US soldier receives attention from an army medic on Utah Beach.

◆ Tiger tank belonging to *SS-Leibstandarte Adolf Hitler* takes up position in the Normandy village of Morgny, 1944. The men of the *Leibstandarte* would prove a formidable opponent to the Allies.

◗ Free French General Charles de Gaulle receives an enthusiastic welcome in the town of Bayeux, June 1944. He arrived in France on 14 June, one week after D-Day, and four years since he last set foot on French soil.

➥ British patrol moves cautiously through the woods of the Bois de Bavent in northern France, June 1944. The soldier on the right is armed with a Sten gun, a cheap, simple weapon that was nevertheless highly effective.

◆ The RAF pounds German positions to the north of Falaise, June 1944. The Allies trapped over 60,000 German troops in the country to the south of Falaise in what would become known as the 'Falaise pocket'.

➥ Infantry of the US 9th Division outside the French town of Lessay, July 1944. The soldier in the foreground is preparing to launch a grenade.

⬆ US soldiers battle for the streets of a town in Normandy, July 1944.

⬇ The liberation of Falaise: locals form an impromptu welcome party for the advancing Allied soldiers.

◆ Dodging bullets in Paris during the uprising, begun on 19 August.

◆ On the barricades: Parisians take up arms, 19 August 1944. Less than one week later, the commander of Paris Major General Dietrich von Choltitz, to his everlasting credit, surrendered the city rather than destroy it as per Hitler's orders.

➥ *Kamerad*: nervous-looking Werhmacht soldiers are marched off into captivity by US troops, under the gaze of escorting civilians.

➥ The other side of liberation: 'Collaborators' – women who have slept with, or are suspected of sleeping with – German soldiers, their heads shaven to indicate this, are jeered through the streets of Paris.

➥ 15 September 1944: British Sherman tanks move up into the Arras area, scene of tank battles against the Germans in 1940. This time, resistance is less.

➡ A bridge too far: glider-borne British paratroops of 1st Airborne Division prepare to go into action at Arnhem, 17 September 1944. Although Colonel John Frost's 2nd Parachute Battalion captured and held the bridge for three days, they were simply too few to hold off the German II SS Panzer Corps.

🡄 US troops of the 82ⁿᵈ Airborne Division during the 'Battle of the Bulge' December 1944–January 1945, an attempt by German Panzer divisions to break through the US lines in the Ardennes and regain the initiative. The attack failed.

🡆 US artillery unit opens fire amidst the Ardennes snow.

◀ German infantrymen move up into the Ardennes Forest, past a line of burning Allied vehicles.

➡ German Tiger tank, knocked out around the Bastogne area in the Ardennes.

✦ Mobile US anti-aircraft unit, France 1945.

✦ US Sherman tanks advance through France on their way to the Rhine, 1945.

▲ US GI takes the enemy in his sights, Cologne, March 1945.

▼ The capture of Cologne: residents of the city extend a cautious welcome to US troops, 7 March 1945.

☚ US Sherman tank amidst the ruins of Aachen, Germany.

☚ Yalta Conference

◆ Units of the US Seventh Army crossing the Rhine near Manheim, March 1945.

◆ Mass grave at Belsen concentration camp, discovered by troops of the British 11ᵗʰ Armoured Division, April 1945. [Author's note: the atrocities of the Third Reich are well documented: any attempt at comment in a book of this nature can only serve to trivialise the subject.]

➡ Where are you? Notices on board seeking information about friends and family, Germany, 1945.

◀ US and Soviet troops meet on the Elbe, May 1945. Although the scene is a somewhat staged photo-opportunity, the emotion displayed by the soldiers, who have just fought their way across the Third Reich, is genuine enough.

◆ Nazis Quit! Soldiers of the US Ninth Army read the good news in the army newspaper *Stars and Stripes.*

➤ On trial at Nuremberg: the Allied War Crimes Tribunal gets underway.

Of the twenty-one defendants, three were acquitted, including former Chancellor of Germany Franz von Papen; seven, including Admirals Raeder and Dönitz, were given prison terms ranging from ten years to life. Ten defendants, including Keitel and Jodl were hanged on 16 October 1946. Herman Göring, also sentenced to death, committed suicide by poison before his turn came around.

4. The Pacific November 1943–August 1945

Between November 1943 and February 1944 US troops recaptured the Gilbert and the Marshall Islands, including Tarawa, Roi and Namur, Makin and Eniwetok. The Japanese defenders fought to the death in nearly all cases. In June 1944 Admiral Spruance, in charge of the fleet protecting the US invasions of Guam and the Marianas Islands, won a decisive victory over the Japanese fleet in the Battle of the Philippine Sea, and the Japanese navy was finished off in the Battle of Leyte Gulf, ending in December 1944. This left the US in complete control of the Philippine Sea. In Burma, the British Fourteenth Army under General William Slim had resisted the Japanese attempts to capture Imphal and Kohima in eastern India, and by the end of 1944 the Japanese were in retreat. The British were poised for an attack through central Burma. Slim's Fourteenth Army pushed down through Burma, retaking Mandalay in February 1945, and Rangoon on 3 May. Although elements of the Japanese Army under Kimura held out until August, the war in Burma was effectively over.

The fighting for the Philippines, like that for the Marshall and Gilbert Islands, was bitter, with elements of the Japanese Army holding out until after the Japanese surrender. Manila on Luzon finally fell on 3 March. Iwo Jima and Okinawa fell between February and June 1945, but Japanese troops held out with such suicidal dedication that the Americans were reluctant to commit themselves to a full invasion of the Japanese mainland, reckoning on 35 per cent casualties as on Okinawa – an amount equal to the entire war dead and wounded of the US to that date. It was with these statistics in mind that Harry Truman, President since the death of Franklin Roosevelt on 12 April, sanctioned use of the atom bomb. On 6 August the first bomb, 'Little Boy', was dropped on Hiroshima, followed by the second, 'Fat Man' on Nagasaki on 9 August. The casualty total of these two 'super-weapons' was around 100,000. On 14 August, Emperor Hirohito addressed the Japanese nation on the radio, urging them to accept not 'surrender', which he avoided mentioning, but the 'coming of peace'. On 2 September, witnessed by representatives from the United States, Britain, the Soviet Union, China, France, Australia, New Zealand and Canada, the delegation from Japan signed the peace treaty and ended the most destructive war in human history.

◗ Sherman tank with supporting infantry moves into action on Bougainville, Solomon Islands, November 1943.

◆ US soldiers armed with flamethrowers assault a Japanese position on Kwajalein Island, February 1944.

◗ US aircraft carrier
USS *Intrepid*
underway in
January 1944.

◆ Gunboats of the US Navy lay smoke in preparation for the landings on Leyte, 20 October 1944.

◆ US troops of 7th Infantry Division on Leyte.

B-17 flies sortie over Luzon in the Philippines.

4th Marine Division storm ashore on Iwo Jima, February 1945.

☞ Forward command post of 4th Marines, Iwo Jima.

☞ Japanese kamikaze attack on US landing craft off Okinawa, 1945.

▶ The USS *Bunker Hill*, Admiral
Spruance's flagship, burns after
Japanese suicide attack, Okinawa,
March 1945. Kamikaze pilots, (the
word means 'Divine Wind'), would
inflict large numbers of casualties on
the US forces during the Okinawa
campaign.

☛ US LCI launches rocket attack as the US Tenth Army prepares to invade Okinawa, 31 March 1945.

◆ Marines await the result of an explosive charge tossed into a Japanese cave position, Okinawa, April 1945.

◆ 5th Marines battle for a ridge north of Naha on Okinawa, May 1945. The ferocity of the fighting on Okinawa convinced the US that a similar invasion of the Japanese mainland would yield an horrific casualty rate. This fact played a part in the American decision to drop the atomic bomb on Japan.

▶ MacArthur returns
to the Philippines,
March 1945, as
promised.

☛ Major General William Slim, whose Fourteenth 'the forgotten' Army drove the Japanese out of Burma, in conversation with Air Marshal Vincent and General Chambers at Government House in Rangoon, August 1945.

☛ Japanese surrender aboard the USS *Missouri*, 2 September 1945. The Second World War is over.

Picture Credits

All photos © Robert Hunt Picture Library, London except: pp. 6, 7 (both), 8 (bottom), 70 (both), 22 (right centre), 29 (both), 33. 37 (bottom), 38, 40, 53, 54 (both), 60 (both), 61 (bottom), 66, 68 (both), 74 (bottom), 78, 79 (bottom), 81 (top), 83 (main), 84, 86 (top), 89, 98 (bottom), 100 (bottom), 101 (top), 112 (bottom), 114 (both), 115 (main & bottom), 124 (top), 125 (top), 126 (all), 127 (centre), 128 (bottom right), 129 (bottom), 130, 140 (top right), 142 (top), 145 (bottom), 146 (both), 147 (bottom), 148, 149, 150 (both), 158 © Hulton Getty Images Ltd

pp. 121 (top), 144 (both), 145 (top), 151, 152 (top) courtesy of the United States Army Military History Institute